Dear Parent:
Your child's love of reading starts here!

Every child learns to read in a different way and at his or her own speed. Some go back and forth between reading levels and read favorite books again and again. Others read through each level in order. You can help your young reader improve and become more confident by encouraging his or her own interests and abilities. From books your child reads with you to the first books he or she reads alone, there are I Can Read Books for every stage of reading:

SHARED READING
Basic language, word repetition, and whimsical illustrations, ideal for sharing with your emergent reader

BEGINNING READING
Short sentences, familiar words, and simple concepts for children eager to read on their own

READING WITH HELP
Engaging stories, longer sentences, and language play for developing readers

READING ALONE
Complex plots, challenging vocabulary, and high-interest topics for the independent reader

ADVANCED READING
Short paragraphs, chapters, and exciting themes for the perfect bridge to chapter books

I Can Read Books have introduced children to the joy of reading since 1957. Featuring award-winning authors and illustrators and a fabulous cast of beloved characters, I Can Read Books set the standard for beginning readers.

A lifetime of discovery begins with the magical words **"I Can Read!"**

Visit www.icanread.com for information
on enriching your child's reading experience.

Ree Drummond and Diane deGroat gratefully acknowledge the editorial and artistic contributions of Amanda Glickman and Rick Whipple.

I Can Read Book® is a trademark of HarperCollins Publishers.

Charlie the Ranch Dog: Stuck in the Mud Text copyright © 2015 by Ree Drummond. Cover art copyright © 2015 by Diane deGroat. Interior art copyright © 2015 by HarperCollins Publishers. All rights reserved. Printed in the United States of America. No part of this book may be used or reproduced in any manner whatsoever without written permission except in the case of brief quotations embodied in critical articles and reviews. For information address HarperCollins Children's Books, a division of HarperCollins Publishers, 195 Broadway, New York, NY 10007.
www.icanread.com

Library of Congress catalog card number: 2014943082
ISBN 978-0-06-234775-6 (trade bdg.)—ISBN 978-0-06-234774-9 (pbk.)

15 16 17 18   PC/WOR   10 9 8 7 6 5 4 3 2   ❖   First Edition

CHARLIE
the Ranch Dog
STUCK IN THE MUD

based on the CHARLIE THE RANCH DOG books
by REE DRUMMOND, The Pioneer Woman,
and DIANE deGROAT

HARPER
An Imprint of HarperCollinsPublishers

Wake up, wake up!

I race around the ranch house.

Get out of bed!

It's time to go out to the pasture.

Hang on.

I better eat just a bit more breakfast.

Moving cattle is a big job.

I'll need my strength.

I run down the porch steps
and Mama helps me into
the back of the truck.
We're on our way!
The air is crisp. The sky is blue.
My tongue goes flap, flap, flap.

Sniff, sniff.

I smell the cows far away
across the green grass.

Did you know

not every dog can be a cattle dog?

In the middle of a herd of cattle,

some dogs get a little crazy.

They chase.

They bark.

They run in circles.

Not me.

No way.

I stay calm, cool, and collected.

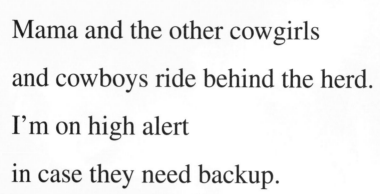

Mama and the other cowgirls
and cowboys ride behind the herd.
I'm on high alert
in case they need backup.

I spot a small calf.

Her name is Abigail.

Look out!

She starts to stray.

I speed up just enough
to put a little pressure on Abigail.
See?
She heads right back to the herd.

Huh?

Hey!

Get back here!

Okay, that's it.

Chase time!

I weave and bob here and there,

under one heel,

then the other.

I am the greatest cattle dog

this ranch has ever seen!

Abigail runs faster and faster.

I'll catch her.

I'm fast.

I'm clever.

I'm focused.

I'm . . .

stuck.

The mud is thick and gooey.

"Lift!" I tell my legs.

They weigh a hundred pounds.

They won't budge!

Don't worry, Abigail!

I'll get us out of this mess.

A cattle dog never panics.

This is no big deal.

We'll be just fine.

My long, floppy ears feel sticky.

Mud is everywhere!

I shake my head to get it off.

Ouch! My eyes!

It stings!

I smell Abigail nearby.

I try to lean a little closer.

Plop!

I fall face first.

Sniff, sniff.

All I smell is a nose full of mud!

RRRRRRROOOOWWOOOOOH!

Where am I?

Someone scratches behind my ears.

I hear Mama's voice.

She cleans my eyes.

I see Mama!

And Abigail.

She's free!

My howl!

It must have done the trick.

Even when I can't move,

can't see,

and can't even smell,

I never lose my cool.

There's no cattle dog like me.

Oh, wonderful, warm, dry ranch house.

Mama hops out of the truck.

No!

Not the hose!

I hate baths.

But I hate mud more.

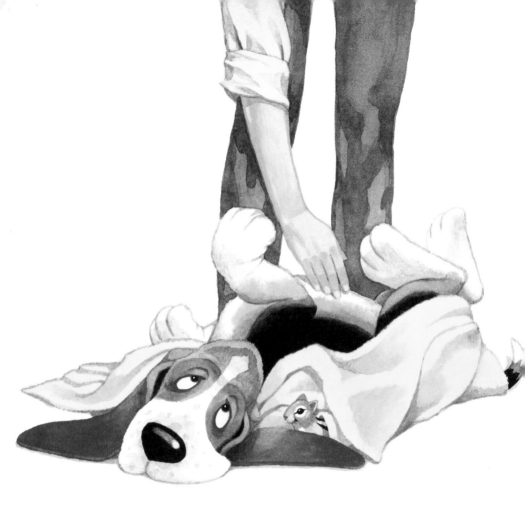

Mama wraps me in a fluffy towel.

I roll on my back.

I'll take a belly rub, please.

And an extra strip of juicy bacon

just for saving the day.